THE FORGIVENESS CHALLENGE

Daily Devotional

BY

DANNY MCKAY

THE FORGIVENESS
CHALLENGE

The Forgiveness Challenge: Daily Devotional

ISBN 978-0-09906701-7-9
Mount Dora, Florida
www.TheForgivenessChallenge.org

CONTENTS

LETTER FROM THE AUTHOR

40 Day Challenge

Colossians 4:2 "Continue earnestly in prayer, vigilant in it with thanksgiving;"

In this book, you will be encouraged to embrace specific activities, prayer, praise & worship, meditation and even fasting (in your own way-"from something for something"). The goal is to devote an hour to developing your relationship with God Almighty through these activities, and track your success through journaling daily events and writing down your successes as well as your testimonies. Each day, you will be given ideas for prayer, devotion and words of encouragement!

Positive change requires positive action, so through daily prayer, honoring God and receiving positive affirmation by words of encouragement, expect a lasting positive change to be ignited in you as you begin on a journey that leads to victory and to you ultimately becoming an overcomer! As Colossians 4:2 reminds us, prayer is the key to starting the fire and our vigilance keeps it!

INTRODUCTION

Why This Book?

The reason I wrote this book is to help anyone who is struggling to overcome any type of issue or circumstance. As our foundation, I present to you a biblically based Divine example of an Overcomer ---- Jesus Christ! He is our model.

Jesus was in the wilderness 40 days praying and fasting. We find an account of this powerful 40 day journey where Jesus had to overcome a great enemy(Satan) in the Gospels of Luke and Matthew (Luke 4:1-13 and Matthew 4:1-11). Jesus met Satan face-to-face and met every challenge that was placed in front of him. Jesus was magnificently victorious! We too can overcome similar obstacles and be victorious. We are not Jesus, but we can follow His example and defeat the enemy, which I believe is the source of many challenges we face.

Overcoming means we no longer allow that negative thing to have control of our lives and manipulate us in almost every move we make. To overcome, we also have to release those bad habits (lack of regular prayer or focused time growing our relationship with the Creator etc.) and replace them with Godly habits. For the next 40 days, we will pursue a meaningful relationship with the Creator and continue to grow strong.

After the 1st 40 days, you will maintain that good habit of daily prayer! The goal is to simply help you take your life back by making positive changes and allow God Almighty to be in control. The secret to our surrender includes letting the Holy Spirit of God guide us in conquering unforgiveness. The goal is to seek and listen for the voice of God.

The problem or circumstance might not go away entirely, but with God in charge, at the very least, you will gain peace, develop trust, grow in strength and have the opportunity to completely overcome your challenge. This book will help you finally stop being a victim of unforgiveness and put you on the road to victory!

Throughout this process, you will experience a new change in that you've set out on a journey where you have supernatural power and heavenly assistance. You are embarking on a 40 day journey that you can carry into the rest of your life where you have access to the resources of a sovereign and divine Lord. God is in charge, because you have surrendered everything to Him. This book helps you get on a path that will lead you to becoming an overcomer by first surrendering your life (or resubmitting your life) to Christ Jesus as your Savior, placing your trust in Him, and putting God firmly in control of every aspect of your life. He will become an integral part of everything you do daily, as you become disciplined incorporating the essential elements of prayer, devotion, studying, praise & worship, meditation, etc.

10 Essential Daily Activities During the Challenge:

1. **Communicate your cares, concerns and requests to God through daily prayer.** I suggest one to two hours per day, or as needed. Just as we eat three times a day, consider feeding yourself spiritually three times a day. Developing a strong relationship with God requires you to talk to Him often. In your prayers, remember to include others that are facing challenges also.

2. **A personalized plan for Prayer-guided Fasting:** This is a personal choice to fast from something for something purposeful to you. For example, fasting from social media, secular music, Internet, TV, food, your favorite hobby, etc. If fasting from food, please be sure to consult a doctor prior to beginning a fast.

3. **Praise & Worship God in a method and style of your choosing, showing gratefulness for what He has already done and is doing.**

4. **Celebrate your victories --- big or small.** Blow your horn! Share your successes.

5. **Meditation/Reflection & Self-Examination Journaling your daily activities, challenges and feelings will help with this.**

6. Devotional time dedicated to strengthening your relationship with God Almighty. This includes studying/reading the Holy Bible and other Christ-centered reading materials.

7. Giving Back – In some way each day, find someone to step outside of your life to help others. This takes the emphasis off of yourself, and reminds you that you have value that others can benefit from. Doing this allows you to invest your time, talent and treasure to help the Kingdom of God. This can be done in a church, your local community, a senior citizen center, youth group, etc. The goal of this is for you to help others in need.

8. Speak positive affirmations and words of encouragement over yourself and others.

9. Do something special to improve how you care for your physical body, which the Bible says is God's temple. You are beautifully and wonderfully made. Some steps you can take toward improving how you take care of your body include better nutrition and diet, exercise, massage, spa, etc.

10. Consider the gifts that God has given you and strive to exercise them and fully utilize them more than you have before. For example, lend your gift by volunteering or mentoring, creating or sharing to honor what God has done for you.

In doing these ten activities each day, I am convinced that if we shoot for the moon, the worse we can do is hit the stars!

Tips For Success With The 40-Day Challenge

I want you to be fully equipped for this remarkable journey, so be encouraged. If you follow these tips, you will be well on your way to victory.

1. **Use the ideas and topics offered for daily prayer, devotional subjects, etc.**

2. **Journal at the end of each day.**

3. **If you want to start a group and do this as a group, or with a significant other, that is also an excellent way to travel on this journey.**

4. **Use the above checklist as a guide.** Do the activities listed and remain open and optimistic, as our Lord leads you!

Getting Started: The Overcomer's Journey

Putting on The Whole Armor of God

Ephesians 6:10-11

"Finally, my brethren, be strong in the Lord and in the power of His might. Put on the whole armor of God, that you may be able to stand against the wiles of the devil."

Forgiveness: Starting Fresh, Clean & New

"And forgive us our sins; for we also forgive everyone that is indebted to us." Luke 11:4

Let's pray so you can get help to forgive, heal and live victoriously!

Example Prayer:

"Heavenly Father, Lord God Almighty, I invite you on this journey with me and surrender my daily schedule to you. Lord guide my actions according to thy will. Oh God, I ask you to forgive me and help me to forgive others of their trespasses against me. Heavenly Father, show me how to be a better person and live righteously. Thank you. I pray in Jesus name. Amen."

Journal your thoughts and reflections:

The Serenity Prayer

Author unknown

God grant me the serenity to accept the things that I cannot change, The courage to change the things that I can, The wisdom to know the difference.

As an Overcomer, you need this prayer for "right" thinking! The key in this prayer is to seek God's guidance. We cannot fail when we listen to the voice of God in every aspect of our lives. If we allow Him, He always leads us in the path of righteousness.

Lessons From David, The Overcomer

PSALM 51: 1 – 19 Written by King David

Have mercy upon me, O God, according to thy lovingkindness: according unto the multitude of thy tender mercies blot out my transgressions.
2 Wash me throughly from mine iniquity, and cleanse me from my sin.
3 For I acknowledge my transgressions: and my sin is ever before me.
4 Against thee, thee only, have I sinned, and done this evil in thy sight: that thou mightest be justified when thou speakest, and be clear when thou judgest.
5 Behold, I was shapen in iniquity; and in sin did my mother conceive me.
6 Behold, thou desirest truth in the inward parts: and in the hidden part thou shalt make me to know wisdom.
7 Purge me with hyssop, and I shall be clean: wash me, and I shall be whiter than snow.
8 Make me to hear joy and gladness; that the bones which thou hast broken may rejoice.
9 Hide thy face from my sins, and blot out all mine iniquities.
10 Create in me a clean heart, O God; and renew a right spirit within me.
11 Cast me not away from thy presence; and take not thy holy spirit from me.

12 Restore unto me the joy of thy salvation; and uphold
me with thy free spirit.
13 Then will I teach transgressors thy ways; and
sinners shall be converted unto thee.
14 Deliver me from bloodguiltiness, O God, thou God
of my salvation: and my tongue shall sing aloud of
thy righteousness.
15 O Lord, open thou my lips; and my mouth shall
shew forth thy praise.
16 For thou desirest not sacrifice; else would I give it:
thou delightest not in burnt offering.
17 The sacrifices of God are a broken spirit: a broken
and a contrite heart, O God, thou wilt not despise.
18 Do good in thy good pleasure unto Zion: build thou
the walls of Jerusalem.
19 Then shalt thou be pleased with the sacrifices of
righteousness, with burnt offering and whole burnt
offering: then shall they offer bullocks upon thine
altar.

David had errored greatly but he came to God in prayer and was specific in his multiple requests. Foremost, he asked for mercy and forgiveness, and acknowledged his sin. He repented, sought God's guidance and accepted God's judgement! David is a perfect model for the Overcomer that seeks victory in sincerity!

The Challenge:
Day 1 - 39

Day 1:
Struggling with Forgiveness

"And whenever you stand praying, if you have anything against anyone, forgive him that your Father in heaven may also forgive you your trespasses. But if you do not forgive, neither will your Father in heaven forgive your trespasses." Mark 11:25-26

Example Prayer:

"Oh Heavenly Father, God Almighty, I ask you to forgive me. I am very sorry and repent for not forgiving others and I apologize for my actions and please help me never to do this again. Lord, I forgive _____________ for the things that were done to me. I pray that _____________ will forgive me also. Heavenly Father, show me how to be a better person and live righteously. Thank you. I pray in Jesus' name. Amen."

Your personal reflections and meditations:

Congratulations on taking the most important step --- the first step. Welcome to the Overcomer's journey!

Day 2:
Worry and Doubt

"Now faith is the substance of things hoped for, the evidence of things not seen." Hebrews 11:1

Let's pray so you can get help to end worry and doubt, and live victoriously!

Example Prayer:

"Heavenly Father, God Almighty, I am sorry for letting worry and doubt overcome me. Oh God, I ask you to strengthen me and help me to have great faith. Help me to focus daily on the positive things in my life by reading and studying your Word. Heavenly Father, show me how to be a better person and live righteously. Thank you for being on this journey with me. I pray in Jesus' name. Amen."

Your personal reflections and meditations:

It is your time to shine.
Don't worry. Be happy!

Day 3: Assurance of God's love and protection

"The LORD is my shepherd; I shall not want. He makes me to lie down in green pastures; He leads me beside the still waters. He restores my soul; He leads me in the paths of righteousness for His name's sake. Yea, though I walk through the valley of the shadow of death, I will fear no evil; for you are with me; Your rod and Your staff, they comfort me. You prepare a table before me in the presence of my enemies; You anoint my head with oil; my cup runs over. Surely goodness and mercy shall follow me all the days of my life; And I will dwell in the house of the LORD Forever." Psalm 23:1-6

Let's pray so you can get reassurance of God's love and protection as you live victoriously!

Example Prayer:

"Oh Heavenly Father, God Almighty, help me to know that you are my Shepherd and all your promises are for me! Thank you Heavenly Father. In Jesus' name I pray. Amen."

Your personal reflections and meditations:

Great things are on the way.
I know you'll never be the same!

Day 4:
Seeking in whom to trust

"Trust in the LORD with all your heart, and lean not on your own understanding; In all your ways acknowledge Him, and He shall direct your paths." Proverbs 3:5

Let's pray so you can maintain your strong faith, grow and live victoriously!

Example Prayer:

"Heavenly Father, God Almighty, I admit that too often I fail to trust you and your Word. In times when I want things to be answered quickly, my trust is so weak. Help me to maintain my trust and faith in you no matter what the circumstances or situations happens to be. I ask you to forgive me and help me never to do this again. In Jesus' name I pray. Thank you. Amen."

Your personal reflections and meditations:

Thank you for trusting!
Trust opens up a beautiful reality.

Day 5:
God's got it! He's in control.

"And we know that all things work together for good to those who love God, to those who are the called according to His purpose." Romans 8:28

Let's pray so you can get help to know that God is always working things out for our good, so that we can heal and live victoriously!

Example Prayer:

"Heavenly Father, God Almighty, I thank you for being God all by yourself. Help me to overcome my unbelief and doubts. I am very sorry and I apologize for my actions. Oh God, I also ask you to forgive me and help me never to do this again. Heavenly Father, show me how to be a better person and live righteously. Thank you. In Jesus' name I pray. Amen."

Your personal reflections and meditations:

He is working for your good…every time!

Day 6:
Desiring peace in your home

"Peace I leave with you, my peace I give unto you. Let not your heart be troubled, neither let it be afraid." John 14:27

Let's pray so you can get the peace that you desire in your home and live victoriously!

Example Prayer:

"Heavenly Father, God Almighty, I ask for peace in my home and in every area of my life. Help me to be peaceful with my family members. Lord let me be a role model of peace. When I have failed, forgive me. I am very sorry and I apologize for my actions. Help me never to do this again. Heavenly Father, show me how to be a better person and live righteously. Thank you. In Jesus' name I pray. Amen."

Your personal reflections and meditations:

Oh how sweet it is --- the Peace of the Lord!

Day 7: Addiction

"If the Son therefore shall make you free, ye shall be free indeed." John 8:36

Let's pray so you can get help to forgive, heal and live victoriously!

Example Prayer:

"Heavenly Father, God Almighty, I need deliverance and freedom from my addiction. Forgive me for my sins! Oh God, I know that you and the power of your Holy Spirit can give me the freedom that I desire. My hope and trust is in you. I surrender to you to lead and guide me to deliverance and freedom. Heavenly Father, show me how to be a better person and live righteously. In Jesus' name I pray. Thank you. Amen."

Your personal reflections and meditations:

Step away from that dark place and
see yourself dancing in the Sunshine!
Freedom, freedom, freedom!

Day 8:
New Start and New Beginning!

"Therefore, if anyone is in Christ, he is a new creation; old things have passed away; behold, all things have become new." II Corinthians 5:17

Let's pray so you can get help to start your new beginning, heal and live victoriously!

Example Prayer:

"Oh Heavenly Father, God Almighty, I have made so many mistakes in my life. Please forgive me! I am very sorry and I apologize for my actions. Oh God, I also ask you to help me start fresh and new in every area of my life. Heavenly Father, show me how to be a better person and live righteously. Thank you for another chance. In Jesus' name I pray. Amen."

Your personal reflections and meditations:

God grants 2nd, 3rd and 4th chances.
He doesn't give up on us!

Day 9:
Who to turn to in tough times

"Do not rejoice over me, my enemy; When I fall, I will rise; When I sit in darkness, the LORD will be a light to me." Micah 7:8

Let's pray so you can get comfort, heal and live victoriously!

Example Prayer:

"Heavenly Father, God Almighty, I have failed greatly in some areas in my life. I want to recover and be restored to my past success and even more. Help me to climb up out of this dark place in my life. I am very sorry and I apologize for my actions. Oh God, I ask you to forgive me and help me never to do this again. Heavenly Father, show me how to be a better person and live righteously. Thank you. In Jesus' name I pray. Amen."

Your personal reflections and meditations:

God has got your back all the time; every time!

Day 10: Struggling with Physical Health

"Beloved, I pray that you may prosper in all things and be in health, just as your soul prospers." III John 1:2

Let's pray so you can get help to heal and live victoriously!

Example Prayer:

"Gracious Heavenly Father, Lord God Almighty, I am struggling with my health. I am facing possible surgery and continuous medical procedures and appointments for many things that are happening to my body. I trust you for my total healing. Give me wisdom, peace and understanding to make right decisions. Please show me how to be a better person and live righteously. In Jesus' name I pray. Thank you. Amen."

Your personal reflections and meditations:

The Lord will make a way out of seemingly no way!

Day 11:
Shedding tears over a deep hurt

Psalms 30:5 "For His anger is but for a moment, His favor is for life; Weeping may endure for a night, but joy comes in the morning."

Let's pray so you can overcome, heal and live victoriously!

Example Prayer:

"Oh Heavenly Father, God Almighty I call on you, Abba Father, seeking forgiveness for my sins. The times I face right now are so very hurtful. I need you, Lord, to help me endure this pain and grief. I hold onto your Word in the Holy Bible to help me be an overcomer, especially in this situation. Lord, please help me to trust you in all things. Heavenly Father, show me how to be a better person and live righteously. In Jesus' name I pray. Thank you. Amen."

Your personal reflections and meditations:

The Lord wipes away all of our tears!

Day 12: Determined to remain steadfast towards goals

Psalms 16:8 "I have set the LORD always before me; because he is at my right hand, I shall not be moved."

Let's pray so you can achieve success, grow and live victoriously!

Example Prayer:

"Heavenly Father, God Almighty, I pray that you will continue helping me to achieve my goals. I know that it is you who has brought me this far and I could not have ever made it if you had not been with me every step of the way. I love you Lord. I am so grateful. Thank you. Oh God, I also ask you to give me opportunities to help other people. Heavenly Father, show me how to be a better person and live righteously. In Jesus' name I pray. Amen."

Your personal reflections and meditations:

Dream big dreams and dare to be a great success!

Jabez The Overcomer

"And Jabez was more honourable than his brethren; and his mother called his name Jabez, saying Because I bare him with sorrow. And Jabez called on the God of Israel, saying, Oh that thou wouldest bless me indeed, and enlarge my coast, and that thine hand might keep me from evil, that it may not grieve me! And God granted him that which he requested." 1 Chronicles 4:9-10

My treasured readers, Jabez did the single most important action ---he prayed to God! Prayer is the key to overcoming any challenge that we face. I believe, that without prayer, there is no true lasting victory! Pray without ceasing!

The Lord's Prayer

"And it came to pass, that, as he was praying in a certain place, when he ceased, one of his disciples said unto him, Lord, teach us to pray, as John taught his disciples. And he said unto them, when ye pray, say Our Father which art in heaven, Hallowed be thy name. Thy kingdom come. Thy will be done, as in Heaven, so in earth. Give us day by day our daily bread. And forgive us our sins; for we forgive every one that is indebted to us. And lead us not into temptation; but deliver us from evil." Luke 11:1-4

"After this manner therefore pray ye; Our Father which art in heaven, Hallowed be thy name. Thy kingdom come. Thy will be done in earth as it is in heaven. Give us this day our daily bread. And forgive us our debts, as we forgive our debtors. And lead us not into temptation, but deliver us from evil: For thine is the kingdom, and the power, and the glory, forever, Amen. Matthew 6:9-13

Day 13: Salvation through Jesus Christ

Acts 2:21 "And it shall come to pass, that whosoever shall call on the name of the LORD shall be saved"

Let's pray so you can receive the gift of salvation!

Example Prayer:

"Heavenly Father, LORD God Almighty, I want to be saved. I am a sinner and repent of my sins. I accept Jesus Christ as my Savior and believe that He died on the cross for me, rose on the third day and is in Heaven with you. I ask you to forgive me, and help me to live a life that is pleasing to you. Thank you for forgiving me of my trespasses and I know you have given me eternal life. Heavenly Father, show me how to be a better person and live righteously. Thank you. In Jesus' name I pray. Amen.

Your personal reflections and meditations:

We have available to us a FREE gift…Eternal Life!

Day 14

I Peter 5:7 "Casting all your care upon him, for he careth for you."

Let's pray so that you can be assured of His love and live victoriously!

Example Prayer:

"Heavenly Father, God Almighty, I thank you for loving and caring for me. Please forgive me of my sins. I am very sorry and I apologize for my actions. I forgive others for their trespasses against me. Oh God, my Heavenly Father, show me how to be a better person and live righteously. Thank you. Amen.

Your personal reflections and meditations:

The Lord cares for you! Oh how He loves you!
When He was on the cross, we were on His mind!

Day 15: Making Critical Decisions in Life

Jeremiah 33:3 "Call unto me, and I will answer thee, and show thee great and mighty things, which thou knowest not."

Let's pray so you know that you can call on the Lord in critical times and get help to make the right decisions.

Example Prayer:

"Heavenly Father, God Almighty, I call upon you to help me make this very critical decision. Lord I need your guidance and pray that you will guide me in the right direction. Oh God, I need you also to forgive me of my sins. Lord help have strong faith and trust in you forever. Heavenly Father, show me how to be a better person and live righteously. Thank you. Amen."

Your personal reflections and meditations:

We are the apple of his eye. He loves us so much!

Day 16:
Desire to draw closer to God

Let's pray so you can get help to forgive, heal and live victoriously!

Example Prayer:

"Heavenly Father, God Almighty, I pray right now for you to take control over my life, including my relationships with family, friends, coworkers etc. I desire to be more like you. Help me to be more patient, kind and courteous. Thank you, Abba Father for answering my prayers. Hallelujah! In Jesus' name I pray. Amen."

Your personal reflections and meditations:

It's okay to lean on Him! He'll never let you fall!

Day 17: Patiently waiting on the Lord to answer prayer

Psalms 27:14 "Wait on the LORD: be of good courage, and he shall strengthen thine heart: wait, I say, on the LORD."

Let's pray so that you will be equipped to wait on the Lord's perfect timing, as He answers your prayers.

Example Prayer:

"Heavenly Father, God Almighty, please help me to have faith, courage and trust in you, that my heart will be strengthened! I admit to often being so impatient. I know you will answer my prayers. You are my Savior and my Lord. Show me how to wait on your answers to my prayers and live righteously. In Jesus' name I pray. Thank you. Amen."

Your personal reflections and meditations:

He gives us the hope to wait on His promises.
He is faithful!

Day 18

John 8:32-36 Freedom is truth! Jesus freedom is freedom indeed!

Let's pray so you can get help to forgive, heal and live victoriously!

Example Prayer:

"Father, God Almighty, I have too many people in my life that are negative and hinder me from doing all I must do to serve you fully. Help me to handle this challenge in my life righteously. I need freedom from drama and negativity. Lord give me the discernment to select equally yoked friends. Thank you. In Jesus' name I pray. Amen."

Your personal reflections and meditations:

I support you breaking away from everything and everyone that does not help you reach your place in God.

Day 19

The Word, the Word. John 1:1-14

Let's pray so you can get help to forgive, heal and live victoriously!

Example Prayer:

"Jesus My Lord, Heavenly Father, God Almighty, I want to have a passionate desire to study and learn of your Word in the Holy Bible. Help me to establish a good pattern of hearing and practicing the Word of God. Abba Father, show me how to walk in your Word and be a better person and live righteously. In Jesus' name I pray. Thank you. Amen.

Your personal reflections and meditations:

Our God will stand for you and defend you!

Day 20

Opening our understanding. Luke 24:36-45.

Let's pray so you can get help to forgive, heal and live victoriously!

Example Prayer:

"Heavenly Father, God Almighty, I have so much to learn and have come a long way. I ask you to continue carrying me further on my journey with you. I want to be a role model for my family to help them grow in faith and strength also. O gracious Heavenly Father, show me through your Word, church, and prayer how to be a better person, gain understanding and live righteously. In Jesus' name I pray. I do Thank you and praise your holy name. Amen."

Your personal reflections and meditations:

I am proud of you! Keep the Faith!

Day 21

Knowing that you too will be with Him in paradise. Luke 23:43

Let's pray so you can get help to forgive, heal and live victoriously!

Example Prayer:

"My Heavenly Father, Lord God Almighty, I want you to help me to be the person that you've intended for me to become. I made mistakes and am sorry and I apologize for my actions. Oh God, I thank you for forgiveness and will never do those things again. Lord, help me, and my family to be forgiving of trespasses and wrong doings. Heavenly Father, show me how to be a better person and live righteously. In Jesus' name I pray. Thank you. Amen."

Your personal reflections and meditations:

You are making the effort to enjoy positive change!

Day 22: Too busy. Too, too busy and feeling stretched very thin

Example Prayer:

"Heavenly Father, God Almighty, I come to you right now, seeking help in organizing my life so that I have smart established priorities and good order. Lord, help me to remove those things that hinder me and replace them with the good Godly things that help improve my life. Heavenly Father, show me how to be a better person, kind and patient. I desire to live righteously. Thank you. In Jesus' name I pray. Amen."

Your personal reflections and meditations:

This is a great day! It is a gift!
You are alive and well!

Day 23: Holy Ghost strength to do your very best every day

Example Prayer:

"Heavenly Father, God Almighty, I seek guidance from you on how to be a better person and live righteously. I want to study the Holy Bible more. I believe that the Holy Spirit will lead me to gain a greater understanding and empower me to do the things that you have purposed in my life. Through my prayers and studying your Word, I ask you to help me overcome my failures. In Jesus' name I pray. Thank you. Hallelujah. Amen."

Your personal reflections and meditations:

Aim high, run hard, and finish strong!

Day 24

Avoid the root of bitterness. Hebrews 12:15

Let's pray so you can get help to forgive, heal and live victoriously!

Example Prayer:

"Heavenly Father, God Almighty, I have been hurt and become disappointed with family and friends. I have become angry too often. I am very sorry and I apologize for my actions. Oh God, I also ask you to forgive me. I have forgiven those that caused me to become angry, but Lord I want to avoid bitterness. I do not want to become bitter. I want to become better! Thanks for my Pastor a nd Bible Teacher. Heavenly Father, please continue to show me how to be a better person and live righteously. Thank you. Amen."

Your personal reflections and meditations:

You are doing great!

Day 25

What is that in your hand? Exodus 4:2 Use what God has given you!

Example Prayer:

"Abba, Heavenly Father, God Almighty, I need you daily. Please show me how to best utilize my gifts, talents and abilities. I want to maximize that which you have placed in my hands and live righteously. Jesus, I give you honor and glory. Thank you. In Jesus' name I pray. Amen."

Your personal reflections and meditations:

You are terrific. Great progress!

Day 26: Financial Success

God's Plan - Jeremiah 29:11-13

Let's pray so you can get help to continue success and live victoriously!

Example Prayer:

"Heavenly Father, God Almighty, I have found some success in my life. I desire to have more success, and seek your guidance to use my success for your Kingdom. I give you all the praise and glory, Lord God. Heavenly Father, show me how to use my success to be a better person and live righteously. Let me be a giver to those in need! Thank you. In Jesus' name I pray. Amen."

Your personal reflections and meditations:

Yeah! Go ahead and get excited!

Day 27

Jesus does not condemn us when others might! John 8:10-11

Let's pray so you can get help to forgive, heal and live victoriously!

Example Prayer:

"Creator of Heaven and Earth, Father, God Almighty, I need to forgive others more quickly and easily, as you forgive me. Help me Lord to not be so slow to extend forgiveness. I need help in NOT condemning others. Thank you for your grace and mercy in my life. I am very sorry and I apologize for my actions. Oh God, I promise not to have this condemning behavior again. Lord please help me to do your will. Father God, show me how to be a better person and live righteously.

Your personal reflections and meditations:

You make it look easy. Grasp onto your victory!

Day 28: Holding on to the progress you've made; not backsliding!

Example Prayer:

"Heavenly Father, God Almighty, I am grateful for the progress that you have allowed me to make in my life. I thank you for helping me to become an overcomer. I give you all praise, honor and glory! My Savior Jesus Christ, I desire to keep going forward on this journey with you. Heavenly Father, show me how to be a better person and live righteously. Thank you. Amen."

Your personal reflections and meditations:

My friend you are earning your victory!

Day 29: Going the extra mile... even if it hurts a bit.

Example Prayer:

"Heavenly Father, God Almighty, I pray that you will give me the energy and strength to keep going strong on this journey. It has been hard at different times. Lord you have come to my rescue time and time again. Thank You! I ask you to strengthen others on this journey with me. O my Heavenly Father, teach me how to climb higher heights and to be a better person and live righteously. Praise and honor and glory go to you. Thank you. Amen."

Your personal reflections and meditations:

Success looks good on you!

Day 30: Admitting wrong when everybody knows anyway

Example Prayer:

"Heavenly Father, God Almighty, I ask you to help me to be reminded to seek forgiveness quickly when I have trespassed against anyone. I pray that my mistakes will not harm anyone. When they do, I want to admit my errors. I seek to quickly forgive others but need help at times. Thank you for being in my life. I love your Word, Lord. Help me to always live righteously. Thank you. Hallelujah! In Jesus' name I pray. Amen."

Your personal reflections and meditations:

This is just what the doctor ordered!

Day 31: Letting go of past hurts and disappointments

Example Prayer:

"Heavenly Father, God Almighty, I have been struggling to let go of past hurts and disappointments. I have sought vengeance when wronged, and know this is not right. Please help me to forgive quickly. O God, I ask you to forgive me and help me never to do this again. Lord help (Name) ____________________ to forgive me of this trespass and wrong. Heavenly Father, show me how to be a forgiving person and live righteously. Thank you. In Jesus' name I pray. Amen."

Your personal reflections and meditations:

Well done! You are in a groove now!

Day 32: Seeking God's Perfect Will

Let's pray so you can get more help to do the will of God!

Example Prayer:

"Heavenly Father, God Almighty, I pray for you to keep guiding me towards your righteousness. I humbly ask you to help me remember to pray about everything and to seek your guidance and wisdom in every area of my life. Lord Jesus, I desire thou perfect Will to be done in my life. I seek your perfect Will to be revealed in my daily prayers. Heavenly Father, show me how to be a better person and live righteously. In Jesus' name I pray. Thank you. Amen."

Your personal reflections and meditations:

I knew you could do it! Impressive!

Day 33: Trying to Become a Great Parent and Spouse

Let's pray so you can get help to achieve this goal, heal and live victoriously!

Example Prayer:

"Heavenly Father, God Almighty, I have been given a good spouse and wonderful children. I know they are gifts from you Lord. At times, I have been impatient with my spouse and too quick to discipline the children. I have spoken harshly too often and failed to say I am sorry. I am very sorry and I apologize for my actions. Oh God, I also ask you to forgive me and help me never to do this again. Lord help my family to forgive me of this trespass and wrong. Heavenly Father, show me how to be a better person, good role model and live righteously. Thank you. Amen."

Your personal reflections and meditations:

Smile you've made great progress!

Day 34: We are the temple of Almighty God and the Holy Spirit

REMEMBER YOU ARE HIS BUILDING
AND WE MUST ALLOW HIM TO SHAPE US.

Let's pray so you can get help to have a stronger faith and live victoriously!

Example Prayer:

"Heavenly Father, God Almighty, I thank you for your Holy Bible and your love for me and my family. I praise you for blessing us daily. It is because of you that I have enjoyed great health and many other blessings. I am grateful for your grace and mercy. Heavenly Father, my prayer is that you will show me how to be a better person. I pray that my actions will reflect the fact that we are the Temple of Almighty God. Oh God, I want to live holy and live righteously. In Jesus' name I pray. Thank you. Amen.

Your personal reflections and meditations:

You are simply amazing!

Day 35: Critical Honesty to Yourself. It's Mirror Time!

Example Prayer:

"Gracious Heavenly Father, I want to ask this prayer for personal honesty. I have discovered that I have been less than honest with myself and others about my actions and behavior. Help me, Lord, to face myself in an honest manner and simply tell the truth! I have hidden too many things from my loved ones. I pray for an honest and sincere spirit. Heavenly Father, show me how to be a better person and live righteously. In Jesus' name I pray. Thank you. Amen."

Your personal reflections and meditations:

Wow! I am not surprised. You are getting it done!
YES!

Day 36: Meditation and Reflection: Your Time to Unwind!

Let's pray so you can get help to make Jesus more of a priority in your life.

Example Prayer:

"Heavenly Father, God Almighty, I pray for a desire to place you in the center of my life and as a priority. I want to pray daily and worship you daily. I want to read and study your Word daily. Lord help me to develop good habits that include you in every aspect of my life. Heavenly Father, show me how to be a better person and live righteously. In Jesus' name I pray. Thank you. Amen."

Your personal reflections and meditations:

Oh Yes! This is a Big Deal! Superb work.

Day 37

Let's pray so you can get help to forgive, heal and live victoriously!

Example Prayer:

"Heavenly Father, God Almighty, I seek wisdom in these challenging times and circumstances for my life. I ask for reconciliation and restoration for every relationship with my children, my siblings and family members. I thank you for bringing me to this place where I have an open, passionate, compassionate and tender heart. Heavenly Father, show me how to be a much better person and live righteously. In Jesus' name I pray. Thank you. Amen."

Your personal reflections and meditations:

Are you really on Day 37? You are serious!
Keep on trucking.

Day 38: Praise & Worship: Vital to Your Christian Relationship

Let's pray so you can be a warrior for the Kingdom of God and live victoriously!

Example Prayer:

"Heavenly Father, God Almighty, I pray for a renewed desire to praise and worship you. I pray for a closer Christian walk with you. I pray for a deeper relationship with you! Heavenly Father, show me how to be a better child of God and live righteously. In Jesus' name I pray. Thank you. Amen."

Your personal reflections and meditations:

It's clear to me. You are a winner!

Day 39

John 14:1-6 Believe in God and let your heart not be troubled

Let's pray so you can get help to forgive, heal and live victoriously!

Example Prayer:

"Heavenly Father, God Almighty, I (hurt, disappointed, failed, wounded etc. (Name) _______________. I am very sorry and I apologize for my actions. Oh God, I also ask you to forgive me and help me never to do this again. Lord help (Name) ____________ to forgive me of this trespass and wrong. Heavenly Father, show me how to be a better person and live righteously. Thank you. Amen.

Your personal reflections and meditations:

Victory is at your fingertips.
Press on towards your prize!

Day 40: Trusting the Creator as Jehovah Jireh, Your Provider!

Example Prayer:

"Heavenly Father, God Almighty, I thank you for my victory. I ask you to forgive me for doubting and help me to never doubt again! I am an Overcomer! I am not a victim! I am a victor! Thank you. Amen."

How do you feel? Journal your personal reflections and meditations:

Beautiful! You are demonstrating the power of faith, trust and hope.

Congratulations!

You have done what Jesus did in Matthew 4 and Luke 4! You made it through the 40 Day Challenge! You are now an overcomer! Well Done! The sun is literally rising on your new beginning. The Lord says, "Well done my good and faithful servant!" I truly believe that now that you've established a very good habit of praying, honoring God with daily devotion and getting those positive words of encouragement. This makes all the difference in the world when trying to deal with overcoming the challenges of life.

It is my prayer that you have been tremendously helped and now you'll never be the same. May I challenge you just a bit further? Jesus told Simon Peter in the Gospel of Luke 22:31-32, "And the Lord said, Simon, Simon, behold Satan hath desired to have you, that he might sift you as wheat: But I have prayed for thee, that thy faith fail not: and when thou art converted, strengthen thy brethren." I know that you have been strengthened by this 40 Day Challenge.

Therefore, my final "challenge", is a humble request for you to go forward and now start helping as many other people as possible with changing their bad habits, like not praying and honoring God on a daily basis. Please give them many words of encouragement and positive affirmations every day, or as often as possible. We both know that daily prayer and honoring God is life changing. It equips us in advance for every trial we might face. May God always richly bless you.

BONUS PRAYERS

PRAYER FOR WHEN I NEED FORGIVENESS

Example Prayer:

"Heavenly Father, God Almighty, I (hurt, disappointed, failed, wounded etc. (Name) ________________. I am very sorry and I apologize for my actions. Oh God, I also ask you to forgive me and help me never to do this again. Heavenly Father, show me how to be a better person and live righteously. Thank you. Amen."

REMEMBERING TO PRAY FOR OTHERS

Example Prayer:

Lord, I include ______________________ in my prayers today. Please help them with ______________________
____
____.

ABOUT THE AUTHOR

Danny McKay is a highly decorated U.S. Navy Iraqi combat veteran, and founder of the Heart Ablaze Church and Bethesda Outreach Ministry in Longwood FL. He holds a Masters Degree of Theology in Biblical Studies from Florida Christian University/ Florida Theological Seminary and currently serves as Vespers Pastor at Carlton Palms Education Center/ADVOSERV, where he also works as a Direct Care Professional for individuals with Developmental Disabilities. He is also the proud Father of three children, Andre, Deanna and Jazmyn. He currently resides in Mount Dora, FL.

To invite **Danny** to your event, visit him on the web at *www.TheForgivenessChallenge.org* or contact him directly at *pastordannymckay@gmail.com.*

CPSIA information can be obtained
at www.ICGtesting.com
Printed in the USA
LVHW041211300720
661941LV00001B/122

9 780990 670179